A WEL
TO A C~~~~~

Four Orders
for Thanksgiving and Blessing

together with
suggestions for hymns and songs

Also included

An Order for the Sacrament of
Holy Baptism of a Child
adapted from *Common Order* for use when both
parents and sponsors participate

and

Vows and Charge to the Congregation
for Use at a Confirmation
(General Assembly 1996)

CHURCH OF SCOTLAND
OFFICE FOR WORSHIP AND DOCTRINE

SAINT ANDREW PRESS
EDINBURGH

First published in 2006 by
SAINT ANDREW PRESS
121 George Street, Edinburgh EH2 4YN

on behalf of the
OFFICE FOR WORSHIP AND DOCTRINE
of the CHURCH OF SCOTLAND

ISBN 10-digit: 0 86153 373 9
ISBN 13-digit: 978 0 86153 373 2

British Library Cataloguing in Publication Data
A catalogue record for this book is available from the British Library

Typesetting by Waverley Typesetters
Printed and bound by Thomson Litho, Glasgow

Contents

Preface

The General Assembly of 2003, having considered the Report of the Panel on Doctrine on Baptism,[1] accepted the need for a ceremony which enabled parents who were not themselves members of the Church to celebrate the gift of a child, whether by birth or adoption. It also noted that there was a greater fluidity of view today about the most appropriate time in a person's life for baptism, and that many Christian parents sought a rite of reception of their child into the family of the Church which would leave the child free upon reaching maturity to decide for him/herself to seek baptism. The General Assembly therefore asked the Panel on Worship to prepare orders which covered these situations.

This booklet includes four such orders. The first and the third are designed to be part of a main diet of Sunday worship, but could also stand alone. The latter is reproduced by permission of the Uniting Church in Australia and appears in that denomination's recently published worship book, *Uniting in Worship 2*. The second is one of many that have evolved in local churches in recent years and have been used within the Sunday morning service.

In the course of the 2003 report, it was noted that the Church today was in a primary missionary situation and that a flexibility of provision would be an advantage. The fourth order is therefore of a less formal kind, suitable for use outwith an act of public worship and in situations where there is little familiarity with the language and formulations of Christian worship.

The opportunity has been taken to include a further order, a modification of the Order for the Holy Baptism of a Child which appears on page 83 of *Common Order*. At the same General Assembly, it was acknowledged that the circumstances of life today could give rise to situations where parents might not be able to commit themselves to bringing a child up within a local

---

1. *Reports to the General Assembly 2003*, 13/1.

congregation but where there were other persons within that congregation who had a significant relationship with the family and who could undertake to keep alive the link between local church and family as the child matured. In the 2005 revision of *Common Order*, space permitted only a small alteration to the Order for the Baptism of a Child, namely a reference to godparents and sponsors in addition to parents. While this makes it possible to use the existing order in these wider circumstances, it was felt important to acknowledge that the parents could retain a significant role not just in the upbringing of the child but also in his/her relationship with all that the Christian faith and the Church stand for. The adaptation printed here addresses this situation.

It is important to note that, in this baptism order, as in the emended Order for Baptism of a Child in *Common Order*, the word 'godparent' does not correspond with the most recent use of this word in the Church of Scotland, where friends of the parents are invited to accompany them but take no part in the ceremony itself, but refers back to an earlier use in the Reformed tradition. There, the godparent took responsibility with the parent for bringing up the child in the Christian faith. Thus it is an alternative term to the word 'sponsor', which is also used in this service and was included for additional clarity of function.

Finally, the General Assembly of 1996, seeking stronger expression of the commitment of those making public profession of faith, and wishing to underline the role of the congregation in a person's development as a disciple of Christ, authorised Questions and a Charge to the Congregation, while not abrogating those already in place. Again, space prevented the inclusion of these in the reprint of the 2005 edition of *Common Order*. They are printed in this booklet and may be substituted for the appropriate sections in *Common Order* (pp. 103 and 117).

Thanks are due to Alan Birss, Peter Donald, Fiona Douglas, Leith Fisher, Joanna Galbraith (Jo Petrie), David S. M. Hamilton, Hugh McGinlay, John McPake and Laurence Whitley, and to my successor in office, Nigel Robb.

September 2005

Douglas Galbraith
Co-ordinator (1995–2005)
Office for Worship and Doctrine
Church of Scotland, wordoc@cofscotland.org.uk

Using these Orders

A service of thanksgiving for or the blessing of a child is sometimes spoken of as an 'alternative' to baptism. There can be, however, no alternative to baptism. Baptism, whether for adults or infants, remains the point of entry into membership of the Church. The four orders which make up the main part of this booklet have a different focus and a different intent, based not on Jesus' own baptism and echoing the many events of and references to baptism in the New Testament but on his loving acknowledgement of children, his blessing of them and his use of them to teach central truths. As a form of worship, they are pastoral, not sacramental. As such, they do not use the language or symbols of baptism, and care should be taken not to 'echo' baptism by the use of the worship space or the gestures employed.

There has been a very long tradition of parents within the Church family bringing their infant children for baptism.[2] Given the current circumstances of shifting patterns and practices, it is hoped that these welcome services will be of use both in pastoral terms and in outreach, and that if good contact is maintained they may lead to the future baptism of these children and to the incorporation of them and their parents into the life of the Church.

There are a number of contexts in which such orders may be found useful.

Parents who do not have a formal link with the Church may seek an opportunity, at the wonder of birth, to express what cannot easily be put into words. They may sense a power greater than themselves and seek in ritual a means of acknowledging this and of expressing in public the hope and the promise they feel. In such circumstances, where baptism

---

2. See Oscar Cullmann, *Baptism in the New Testament*, who argues that it was exceptional *not* to do so.

is not seen as answering the situation, these orders may enable ministers and Kirk Sessions to make a positive response to approaches from such families.

Or, some may simply want to bring their newborn child to church at the first opportunity after birth for him/her to be recognised and welcomed and for the community to give thanks – and perhaps in a particular instance there may be a special reason for giving thanks – as well as to renew their parental commitment before God. Such orders may be of use also in contexts where parents come from different faith communities and neither is free to assent to the requirements of the other. In a different scenario, parents may wish to celebrate the arrival of an adopted child – who may have already been baptised.

Or, some parents who are committed church members may wish to have an act of thanksgiving, apart from baptism, to mark their child's entry into their own family and into the family of the Church, but leave it possible for the child in later years to make his/her own decision about baptism.

There is variety implied in these first four orders, from an informal ceremony at home, in hospital or in some other secular setting, through an event which is part of a service of public worship, to a complete service whose main focus is thanksgiving, blessing and the dedication of parents. Within that, there is scope for even greater variety, the minister having matched the order to the situation and then perhaps made further adaptation – for example, where there is little understanding of the language commonly used in churches, where siblings are present, where the child is no longer an infant, or where there is more than one child to be welcomed. Sometimes a person other than the minister might be the one to preside and give the blessing.

The orders in this booklet may be downloaded from the Worship and Doctrine pages of the Church of Scotland's website, www.churchofscotland.org.uk, and will be added to the CD of the Church's worship publications, now available.

Acknowledgements

The Panel on Worship has appreciated the opportunity of studying orders prepared by other denominations, particularly those in *The Methodist Worship Book* (1999), *Worship from the United Reformed Church* (2003), *Celebrate God's Presence* (United Church of Canada, 2000) and *The Book of Common Worship* (Presbyterian Church of Canada, 1991), among others, of which echoes may occasionally be found.

Scriptural quotations are from the *New Revised Standard Version*, © 1989 Division of Christian Education of the National Council of the Churches of Christ in the United States of America, published by Oxford University Press, and from *The Revised English Bible*, © Oxford University Press/Cambridge University Press, 1989.

The Declaration '*N*, for you Jesus Christ came into the world' in the alternative order for Baptism is adapted from the baptismal liturgy of L'Église Réformée de France.

The extract 'It may sound strange ...' from Henri Nouwen, *Reaching Out* (Collins Fount, 1980), is reproduced by permission of Zondervan.

The extract 'If I had my child ...' from Diane and Julia Loomans, *Full Esteem Ahead: 100 ways to build self-esteem in adults and children* (H. J. Kramer, 1994), is reproduced by permission.

A. Orders for a Welcome to a Child

1
First Order

This order may be used as part of the main Sunday service or on its own on a separate occasion.

Hymn [see section D. Hymns and Songs]

During the singing of the hymn, the family bringing the child may move into seats where the act of welcome may best be conducted.

Introduction

The minister says:

In the Gospel we read:

They brought children for him to touch.
The disciples rebuked them,
but when Jesus saw it he was indignant,
and said to them,
'Let the children come to me;
do not try to stop them;
for the kingdom of God belongs to such as these.
Truly I tell you:
whoever does not accept the kingdom of God like a child
will never enter it.'
And he put his arms round them,
laid his hands on them,
and blessed them.

Mark 10:13–16

Today, gathered as part of the family of God, we are to give thanks with *A* and *B* (parents), and with *C* and *D* (brothers, sisters), for the arrival of their *son and brother/ daughter and sister N*, (and) to ask God's blessing on *N* as *he* grows in faith and understanding (and to declare our love and support for *A* and *B* as they look forward to the delights and commit themselves to the duties of parenthood). Let us pray.

Prayer

The minister says:

God of love, we thank you.
Each day we know your goodness:
in the nourishment of the table,
in the protection of our families,
in the support of our friends,
in the fellowship of our communities.
Especially today we thank you
that out of love you bring new life,
awakening us to new joy and hope,
but offering also new challenge
to the priorities by which we live,
drawing from us reserves
of care, patience and compassion,
and reminding us of how your kingdom
is built from the gifts that children bring
to the life of the world and to our lives.
Bless to us this moment of giving thanks
and of welcoming this child
that we may have a new sense
of the gifts continually lavished upon us:
through Jesus Christ, our Lord.   **Amen.**

Readings

*One or more of these passages is read; they may be
introduced or followed by a brief comment:*

Hear, Israel: the Lord is our God, the Lord our one God;
and you must love the Lord your God with all your heart
and with all your soul, and with all your strength.
These commandments which I give you this day
are to be remembered and taken to heart;
repeat them to your children,
and speak of them both indoors and out of doors,
when you lie down, and when you get up.

Deuteronomy 6:4–7

You it was who fashioned my inward parts;
you knitted me together in my mother's womb.
I praise you, for you fill me with awe;
wonderful you are, and wonderful your works.
You know me through and through:
my body was no mystery to you,
when I was formed in secret,
woven in the depths of the earth.
Your eyes foresaw my deeds,
and they were all recorded in your book;
my life was fashioned
before it had come into being.

Psalm 139:13–17

At that time the disciples came to Jesus and asked,
'Who is the greatest in the kingdom of Heaven?'
He called a child, set him in front of them, and said,
'Truly I tell you: unless you turn round
and become like children,
you will never enter the kingdom of Heaven.

Whoever humbles himself and becomes like this child
will be the greatest in the kingdom of Heaven,
and whoever receives one such child in my name
receives me.'

Matthew 18:1–5

The following are also suitable:

Deuteronomy 31:12–13   *Passing on the traditions*
1 Samuel 1:9–11, 20–28; 2:26   *Samuel's birth and childhood*
Psalm 8   *Humankind, young and old, as part of creation*
Psalm 78:1–7   *Telling each new generation of the love of God*
Psalm 103   *God's compassion is like a parent's*
Psalm 128   *The blessings of a family*
Luke 1:26–38   *Mary learns she is to have a child*
Luke 2:22–32   *Jesus' presentation in the Temple*
Luke 2:33–40, 52   *Simeon and Anna recognise the child Jesus*
Ephesians 3:14–21   *Families in earth and in heaven*
Ephesians 6:1–4   *Parents and children*

Welcome and Blessing

As the child is presented, the minister may hold or touch the child as the blessing is said.

The minister says:

N, through all that life will bring
may God's presence strengthen you,
God's love guide your actions,
God's joy lift your heart.   **Amen.**

The minister says to the parents (and family):

In receiving *N* as a gift from God
and in welcoming *him* into your family,
do you promise so to live your lives
that *he* will grow up surrounded by love and trust?

We do.

If there are older children in the family, the minister may include a suitable promise for them to make.

When the parents are members of the Church but do not ask for baptism at this time, the minister may say:

Do you promise, with God's help,
to provide a Christian home for *N*
and to bring *him* up in the faith of the Gospel
and the fellowship of the Church?

We do.

The minister says to the congregation:

Members of the body of Christ,
will you surround this family with your love,
and support them with your prayers?

We will.

A sign of welcome may be presented by adults or children (see note 7 to the Third Order, page 10).

Closing prayer

Lord Jesus Christ,
who shared in Nazareth the life of an earthly home,
dwell with these parents, this child, and all their family,
leading them in the ways of peace and trust,
love and service.

We pray for *N*, that *he* might know your love
and learn to love your world,
and the whole family of your children.
May *he* in due time come to you in baptism
and make *his* own profession of faith in you.
May all people the world over so value their children
that they seek an end to poverty, disease and fear,
so that all may have an equal chance
of growing to maturity in peace and in plenty;
through Jesus Christ, our Lord.   **Amen.**

*The Lord's Prayer may be said, if not said elsewhere in
the service.*

The service continues.

*If the service is to end here, a hymn or blessing may be
sung (see section D. Hymns and Songs), followed by a
dismissal and benediction.*

2

A Shorter Order

This order forms part of the main Sunday service.

Hymn [see section D. Hymns and Songs]

Introduction

The minister says:

A and *B* have had their lives enriched and blessed by the gift of this child, *N*. Today they have come here to thank God for *his/her* presence and the difference *he/she* has made to their lives.

Also, they have invited us as a congregation to share in their joy and together to ask God's blessing upon *N* and upon them, that they may worthily face the challenges and privileges of parenthood in the years ahead. This we gladly do, in the name of Jesus Christ whose express wish was that children should be brought to him, and not be kept back, that he might lay his hands upon them and bless them.

Let all stand.

Promise and Blessing

The minister addresses the parents:

In recognising the goodness of God in granting you the gift of the child you have brought before him, do you earnestly desire that *he/she* be given Christ's blessing just as he blessed the children long ago, and do you promise that you will be worthy and loving parents as long as *he/she* shall live?

We do.

The minister takes the child and says:

N, in the name of the Lord Jesus Christ, and following his example, I commend you to the gracious care and protection of God through all your days. May his richest blessing rest and abide with you always.

Prayer

The minister says:

Let us pray.

Lord, we pray for this family. In the trials and challenges of parenthood, surround them with your blessing. May they know that you are always there, always ready to love and protect, always able to lift them when cast down and to restore them to sanity and joy. Bless also the parents. Go with them on their walk into the unknown future. Endow them with wisdom, courage and humour, so that with this child, your gift, they may explore with daily increasing wonder the pathways of family life in peace and happiness.   **Amen.**

The congregation may sing a blessing (see section D. Hymns and Songs).[3]

The service continues

---

3. It is suggested that this be other than the Aaronic Blessing, common at Baptism.

A Service of Thanksgiving for and Blessing of a Child[4]

reprinted by permission from Uniting in Worship 2, *the worship book of the Uniting Church in Australia.*

NOTES

1 This service may form part of a normal Sunday service of the congregation; it is placed at an appropriate place between The Preaching of the Word and The Prayers of the People.

2 The order combines thanksgiving for the birth or adoption of a child, the blessing of the child, and the self-dedication of the parent(s) to their task. It is appropriately used on the first occasion on which a child is present in the worshipping community, but it may be delayed, e.g. in order for family members to be present. Part or all of this service may be held in a home or hospital, at the discretion of the minister.

3 Care should be taken so that the service is not confused with baptism, e.g. by not standing near the font.

4 It is appropriate to use this service whether or not it is intended to baptise the child at a later date.

5 If a service of thanksgiving only is desired, the reference to blessing in (2) and the whole of (6) shall be omitted.

---

4. © 2005 The Assembly of the Uniting Church in Australia, used with permission.

6   A parent holds the child throughout the service. If only one parent is present, the wording of this service needs to be suitably amended.

7   An elder or other representative of the congregation may say the response in (8), or similar words. The gift referred to here may be a Bible or New Testament, seeds, a plant or a suitable children's book. A candle should not be presented, as it is a significant part of the service of Baptism.

8   If liturgical colours are used, the colour should be that of the season of the Christian year.

1   **Hymn/Song**

2   **Presentation**

The elder responsible for the care of the family brings the parent(s), the child and any sisters and brothers forward and introduces them to the congregation.

Friends,
I present to you *A* and *B*
who have come to give thanks for their child *N*,
and so that *N* may receive the blessing of God.
(I also present *C* and *D*
who are glad to be welcoming
a new *sister/brother* into their family.)
With them,
we give our thanks to God.

3   **Introduction**

The minister or elder reads one or both of the following:

Jesus said,
'Let the children come to me;
do not try to stop them;
for the kingdom of God belongs to such as these.
Truly I tell you:
whoever does not accept the kingdom of God like a
  child
will never enter it.'
And he put his arms round them,
laid his hands on them,
and blessed them.

Mark 10:14–16

and/or

Hear, Israel: the Lord is our God, the Lord our one
  God;
and you must love the Lord your God with all your
  heart
and with all your soul, and with all your strength.
These commandments which I give you this day
are to be remembered and taken to heart;
repeat them to your children,
and speak of them both indoors and out of doors,
when you lie down, and when you get up.

Deuteronomy 6:4–7

The minister says:

All life is from God,
and children are a gift from the Lord.
Within a family,
the *birth/adoption* of a child
is a joyous and solemn occasion.
In this event we see the wonder
of God's loving creativity among us.

We are now to share the joy of this family
whose life has been enriched
by the gift of *N*.

4 **Psalm**

*The minister, elder or parent(s) may lead the
congregation in a responsive reading, e.g. one or
more of the following. Other suitable psalms include
Psalm 23 or 100.*

God, be gracious to us and bless us
and make your face to shine upon us,
that your way may be known upon earth,
your saving power among all nations.

Let the nations be glad and sing for joy,
for you judge the peoples with equity
and guide the nations upon earth.

Let the peoples praise you, O God;
let all the peoples praise you.

The earth has yielded its increase;
God, our God, has blessed us.
O God, extend your blessing upon us;
may the whole world worship you.

Psalm 67

and/or

O Lord, you have searched me and you know me.
You know me at rest and in action;
you know my innermost thoughts.

You formed my inward parts;
you knitted me together in my mother's womb.

I praise you, for you fill me with awe;
wonderful you are, and wonderful your works.

Wonderful you are, and wonderful your works;
you know me through and through:
my body was no mystery to you,
when I was being made in secret,
and formed in the hidden depths.
Your eyes saw my unformed substance.
In your book were written, every one of them,
the days that were formed for me,
when none of them as yet existed.

How mysterious to me are your thoughts, O God!
How vast is the sum of them!
If I would count them – they are more than the
   sand;
I come to the end – I am still with you.

Psalm 139:1–2, 13–18

5   **Prayer of Thanksgiving**

The minister or elder offers one of the following
prayers and/or free prayer.

Let us pray:

O God,
like a mother who comforts her children,
you sustain, nurture and strengthen us;
like a father who cares for his children,
you look upon us with compassion and goodness.
We give you thanks for the *birth/adoption* of *N,*
and for the joy that has come to this family.
Confirm their joy by a lively sense
of your presence with them.

Give them calm strength and patient wisdom
as they seek to bring this child
to love all that is true and noble,
just and pure,
lovable and gracious,
excellent and admirable,
following the example of our Lord and Saviour,
    Jesus Christ.
Amen.

or

Creator God,
we give you thanks and praise
for the gift of this child.
We thank you for creating *her/him* in your image,
and breathing into *her/him* the breath of life.
We thank you for the love
which these parents have for each other,
and for the welcome they are giving to *N*.
By the power of the Holy Spirit,
fill their home with love, trust and understanding;
through Jesus Christ our Lord.
Amen.

or

God of infancy and age,
God of youth and maturity,
God in our play and our work;
we thank you for the gift of *N*,
who comes to us bearing your image
in *her/his* own way.
We thank you for this family,
and for the love and care given to *N*.
Be with *A* and *B* as they seek to guide *her/him*

in the ways of love and justice,
and strengthen them in the truth and grace
of Jesus Christ our Lord.
Amen.

6   **The Blessing of the Child**

*The minister may touch the child's head, hands and
feet as indicated.*

May God grant you grace
    to grow in wisdom and understanding,
        (*touch head*)
    to work with Christ for justice in the world,
        (*touch hands*)
    and to walk with the Spirit in the ways of peace;
        (*touch feet*)
and the blessing of the Holy One,
the Father, the Son and the Holy Spirit,
be upon you this day and for evermore.

The people respond:

Amen.

7   **Dedication of the Parents**

The minister addresses the parents:

Do you receive *N* as a gift from God?

One or both parents says one of the following:

**We thankfully receive *N*
as a gift from God.
With humility and hope
we dedicate ourselves
to love and care for *her/him*,**

**and to set before *her/him* the Christian faith
by teaching and example.
In this we ask for the power of the Holy Spirit
and the prayers of the Church.**

or

**We thankfully receive *N*
as a gift from God.
With humility and hope
we dedicate ourselves
to love and care for *her/him*.**

8   **Congregational Response**

The minister says:

The Church is the family of Christ,
the community in which we grow in faith and
     commitment.

The people say:

**We rejoice in God's blessing of *N*.
We seek God's grace to be a community
in which the gospel is truly proclaimed to all.
We will support you and your child,
and pray that through our love
she/he may come to know God's love.**

*A gift from the congregation may be given (see
note 7, page 10).*

9   **Concluding Prayer**

The following prayer and/or free prayer is offered:

Gracious God,
you entrusted your Son Jesus
to the protection and care of Mary and Joseph,
their families and community.
You have now entrusted this child *N* to *her/his*
    family.
Strengthen *A* and *B* by your Holy Spirit,
and help this congregation
to be a caring community in Christ.
May *N* be brought by grace
to the sacrament of baptism,
and come, with all your people,
to the fullness of your kingdom of love and peace;
through Jesus Christ our Lord.
Amen.

10 **Hymn/Song**

*If a hymn/song of praise or thanksgiving was not
sung at the beginning of this service, one may be
sung here.*

4

An Informal Order

Invitation

Family and guests may stand or sit around the room or hall. The parents and child(ren) are grouped together with the minister/person presiding in a central place. The ceremony may be in the context of a party or reception, or it may be held on its own.

The minister or person presiding may say such words as these:

I am sure you all know how welcome you are, and how much *A* and *B* appreciate your coming today to celebrate with them the *birth/adoption* of *N* and to express your support of them in their task as parents. We will be thinking especially about this family, and the extended family to which they belong, but we will also think about children and their families everywhere, many of whom do not know the blessings we enjoy. Sometimes we shall hear readings, sometimes the words will be in the form of prayers or meditations. Feel free to join in in whatever way you wish.

Let's hear some music as we get ready to share in this short ceremony. (*See section D. Hymns and Songs.*)

Scripture Reading

The minister/person presiding may introduce the reading,
which may then be read by a member of the group, in
these or similar words:

One of the most famous passages ever written about
the importance of children is in one of the books of the
Bible, where Jesus loses patience with adults present who
were trying to take up all his attention. He tells them that
everyone, whatever their age, should look at life through
the mind and eyes of a child.

They brought children for him to touch.
The disciples rebuked them,
but when Jesus saw it he was indignant,
and said to them,
'Let the children come to me;
do not try to stop them;
for the kingdom of God belongs to such as these.
Truly I tell you:
whoever does not accept the kingdom of God like a child
will never enter it.'
And he put his arms round them,
laid his hands on them,
and blessed them.

Mark 10:13–16

An Act of Thanksgiving

The minister/person presiding says:

Our main feeling at this time is surely one of gratitude
– gratitude for this new gift of a child and for all the
generosity and skill that accompanied *his* arrival. Let us
be quiet and think about all we have to be thankful for ...

After a short silence:

We give thanks for the wonder of new life,
for the human love out of which it comes.
We celebrate this tiny human form,
the joy brought by a first smile,
a first word and sentence.
We give thanks also for those who bring life forth –
midwives, doctors, nurses, health visitors,
especially those who gave wonderful support
to *A*, *B* and *N* at the time of *his/her* birth.
We remember with gratitude too
the friends and family who supported us,
generous with their gifts and their love.
May we continue to find pleasure
in all the new things our children bring us
as they grow through the years;
and may we show our gratitude
by living our lives in a spirit of thankfulness.
This is our hope and our prayer.

Readings

Use may be made of one or both of the two extracts below, or other readings may be chosen. If more than one faith is represented in the family, a reading from other scriptures could be included. These extracts may be read by others present.

The minister/person presiding introduces the reading:

The arrival of a child causes a big change in the life of a family. This contemporary Christian author looks at the changes we have to make, and says we should look on our children as our most important guests.

It may sound strange to speak of the relationship between parents and children in terms of hospitality. But it belongs to the centre of the Christian message that children are not properties to own and rule over, but gifts to cherish and care for. Our children are our most important guests, who enter into our home, ask for careful attention, stay for a while and then leave to follow their own way.

Children are strangers whom we have to get to know. They have their own style, their own rhythm and their own capacities for good and evil. They cannot be explained by looking at their parents. It is, therefore, not surprising to hear parents say about their children, 'They are all different, none is like the other and they keep surprising and amazing us' ...

Children carry a promise with them, a hidden treasure that has to be led into the open through education ... in a hospitable home. It takes much time and patience to make the little stranger feel at home, and it is realistic to say that parents have to learn to love their children. Sometimes a father or mother will be honest and free enough to say that he or she looked at the new baby as at a stranger without feeling any special affection, not because the child was unwanted but because love is not an automatic reaction. It comes forth out of a relationship which has to grow and deepen....

What parents can offer is a home, a place that is receptive but also has the safe boundaries within which their children can develop and discover what is helpful and what is harmful.

Henri J. M. Nouwen, in *Reaching Out* (Collins Fount, 1980)

The minister/person presiding introduces the reading:

Looking back, we can often see more clearly what we should have done, like this parent.

> If I had my child to raise all over again,
> I'd finger-paint more, and point the finger less.
> I would do less correcting and more connecting.
> I'd take my eyes off my watch, and watch with my eyes.

I would care to know less and know to care more.
I'd take more hikes and fly more kites.
I'd stop playing serious, and seriously play.
I would run through more fields and gaze at more stars.
I'd do more hugging and less tugging.
I'd build self-esteem first, and the house later.
I would be firm less often, and affirm much more.
I'd teach less about the love of power,
and more about the power of love.

Diane Loomans, in *Full Esteem Ahead*

Blessing

The minister/person presiding lays his/her hand on the child(ren). Others may also do so.

N, we will always love you.
May God's blessing be upon you
this day and all the days ahead.
May all that is loving surround you,
all that is strong and true and free walk with you
and your life be filled with joy.

All return to their places.

A song/hymn may be sung, or music played (see section D. Hymns and Songs). If recorded music, it may fade and continue playing under the following prayer/meditation.

The minister/celebrant continues:

Let us now express our hopes for this child, for *his* parents, and for children everywhere.

Our prayer is that *N* may enjoy a childhood
unspoilt by tragedy and free from danger,
until it is time for *him* to go out as an individual,
strong to work for justice,
using *his* talents to bring help and joy to others,
and so find joy *himself*.

May he meet with just treatment on *his* journey,
but if *he* should encounter unfairness
may *he* be able to respond with kindness.
May *he* not be misled by hollow promises,
but always keep hold of important values,
open to development and change within *himself*
and able to enjoy good relationships with other human
    beings.

We are thinking too of his parents,
the patience, strength and love they will need,
and the example they will give;
of the grandparents and wider family,
able to model all that is admirable and gracious;
and of all the friends of the family,
bringing other perspectives and possibilities
to the life of *N* as *he* grows.

Our prayer too is that children everywhere
will be made welcome, fed and cared for,
protected from harm, affirmed and loved.
We remember those who have lost their children
in disaster or through disease or famine,
or who are worried about their health and their future
in a devastated land,
and we pray for all who help them.

May these thoughts and prayers we share come true.
Amen.

The minister/celebrant says:

Now let us hear some music to lead us into the next stage
of our celebration, as we mingle and enjoy each other's
company!

Music is played (see section D. Hymns and Songs).

B. Order for the Sacrament of Holy Baptism

For a Child

This order is for use when parents who are not Church members, or are unable or unwilling to make a confession of faith, are accompanied by a sponsor or sponsors who as members of the Church will make confession of faith and undertake to contribute to the Christian upbringing of the child. It is substantially the same as that in Common Order *(2005) but with additional material which acknowledges that, although they are not themselves asked to take responsibility for bringing their child up within the Church community, the parents may in their own way encourage the Christian upbringing of their child.*

In this order, 'godparent' and 'sponsor' both refer to the person who makes confession and undertakes responsibility. If there are 'godparents' in the newer sense of friends accompanying the parents (see the Preface to this booklet), their role should be confined to 'moral support', and they should not be in close attendance when the godparent/sponsor and the parents make their declarations.

Other members of their families and their district elder may accompany the family seeking baptism.

Normally, the Sacrament is administered during Sunday worship, usually after the sermon.

1 **Words of Institution**

The minister says:

The Gospel tells us that
'Jesus was baptised in the Jordan by John.
As he was coming up out of the water,
he saw the heavens break open
and the Spirit descend on him, like a dove.
And a voice came from heaven;
"You are my beloved Son;
in you I take delight".'

Mark 1:9–11

Jesus himself said:

Full authority in heaven and on earth
has been committed to me.
Go therefore to all nations
and make them my disciples;
baptise them in the name of the Father
and the Son and the Holy Spirit,
and teach them to observe
all that I have commanded you.
I will be with you always, to the end of time.

Matthew 28:18–20

On the Day of Pentecost, the Apostle Peter said:
Repent and be baptised, every one of you,
in the name of Jesus the Messiah;
then your sins will be forgiven
and you will receive the gift of the Holy Spirit.
The promise is to you and to your children
and to all who are far away,
to everyone whom the Lord our God may call.

Acts 2:38–9

In addition, one or more of the following may be read:

Isaiah 43:1–2a   *I call you by name; you are mine*
Ezekiel 36:25a, 26a   *I shall sprinkle pure water over you*
Luke 18:16–17   *Let the children come to me*
John 3:5–7   *You must all be born again*
Romans 6:3–4   *We were baptised unto his death*
Ephesians 4:4–6   *One Lord, one faith, one baptism*
Titus 3:4–7   *He saved us through the water of rebirth*
1 Peter 2:9   *You are a chosen race, a royal priesthood*

2 Statement

The minister says:

When Jesus was baptised
in the waters of the Jordan,
the Spirit of God came upon him.
His baptism was completed
through his dying and rising again.

Our baptism is the sign of dying to sin
and rising to new life in Christ.

It is Christ himself who baptises us.
By the Spirit of Pentecost,
he makes us members of his body, the Church,
and calls us to share his ministry in the world.

By water and the Holy Spirit,
God claims us as his own,
washes us from sin,
and sets us free from the power of death.

In this sacrament,
the love of God is offered to each one of us.
Though we cannot understand or explain it,
we are called to accept that love
with the openness and trust of a child.
In baptism,
N is assured
of the love that God has for *her*,
and the sign and seal of the Holy Spirit
is placed upon *her*.

3 **Confession**

*Where a godparent or sponsor presents the child, the
minister says:*

N, you have come as a member of the Church
to stand alongside these loving parents
at the baptism of their child,
desiring that *she* may be grafted into Christ
as a member of his body, the Church.
Do you receive the teaching of the Christian faith
which we confess in the Apostles' Creed?

I do.

The minister says:

Will the congregation please stand.
Let us affirm the faith.

The Apostles' Creed is said.

4 **Prayer**

The minister says:

Let us pray.

We thank you, gracious God,
for your gifts of water and the Holy Spirit.
[In the beginning, you moved over the waters
and brought light and life to a formless waste.
By the waters of the flood,
you cleansed the world,
and made with Noah and his family
a new beginning for all people.
In the time of Moses, you led your people
out of slavery through the waters of the sea,
making covenant with them in a new land.
At the appointed time,
in the waters of the Jordan
when Jesus was baptised by John,
you sent your Spirit upon him.
And now, by the baptism
of his death and resurrection,
Christ sets us free from sin and death
and opens the way to eternal life.]

The minister may pour water into the font.

Send your Holy Spirit
upon us and upon this water,
that *N*,
being buried with Christ in baptism,
may rise with him to newness of life;
and being born anew of water and the Holy Spirit
may remain for ever
in the number of your faithful children;
through Jesus Christ our Lord,
to whom with you and the Holy Spirit
be all honour and glory, now and for ever.   **Amen.**

5 Declaration

For each child, the minister says such words as:

N, for you Jesus Christ came into the world:
for you he lived and showed God's love;
for you he suffered the darkness of Calvary
and cried at the last, 'It is accomplished';
for you he triumphed over death
and rose in newness of life;
for you he ascended to reign at God's right hand.
All this he did for you, *N*,
though you do not know it yet.
And so the word of Scripture is fulfilled:
'We love because God loved us first'.

6 Baptism

The minister pours or sprinkles water on each child's head, saying:

N, I baptise you
in (*or* into) the name of the Father,
and of the Son,
and of the Holy Spirit.   **Amen.**

7 Blessing

The minister says:

The blessing of God Almighty,
Father, Son, and Holy Spirit,
descend upon you,
and dwell in your heart for ever.   **Amen.**

This blessing may be said or sung:

The Lord bless you and keep you;
the Lord make his face to shine upon you,
and be gracious unto you;
the Lord lift up his countenance upon you,
and give you peace. **Amen.**

The minister says:

N is now baptised into Jesus Christ.
We receive and welcome *her* as a member
of the one holy catholic and apostolic Church.

8 Promise

*The minister addresses parents as well as the
godparent/sponsor:*

This child belongs to God in Christ.
From this day *she* will be at home
in the Christian community,
and there will always be a place for *her*.
Will you together
tell *her* of *her* baptism,
and unfold to *her* the treasure
she has been given today,
so that *she* may know *she* is baptised,
and, as *she* grows,
make *her* own response in faith and love,
and come in due time
to share in the communion
of the body and blood of Christ.

The minister says to the godparent/sponsor:

Today you have presented this child for baptism.
Do you promise in the days and years to come
to pray for *her* and encourage *her*
so that *she* may grow up
in the life and worship of the Church?

  I do.

The minister says to the parents:

A and *B*,
today you have shared in the baptism of your
    child.
Do you promise to cherish *her* and care for *her*,
and so to live your lives and build your home
that *she* will be surrounded by love and
    goodness
throughout *her* growing years?

  We do.

9 **Commitment of Congregation**

The minister says to the congregation:

You who are gathered here
represent the whole Church,
the Church catholic.
Word and Sacrament bring you
the joy of Christ's presence in your midst.
They also bring you responsibilities
as Christ's people in this place.
Do you welcome *N*;
and do you renew your commitment,
with God's help,
to live before all God's children

in a kindly and Christian way,
and to share with them
the knowledge and love of Christ?

The congregation says:

We do.

The minister and congregation say together:

**With God's help
we will live out our baptism
as a loving community in Christ:
nurturing one another in faith,
upholding one another in prayer,
and encouraging one another in service.**

10　**Prayers**

The minister says:

Let us pray.

God of love, we rejoice again
to receive your grace in Word and Sacrament.
We have heard your call
and are made new by your Spirit.

Guide and guard *N* all *her* days.
May your love hold *her*,
your truth guide *her*,
your joy delight *her*.
Bless *her* parents,
that *she* may grow up
in a secure and happy home.
Give to *her* family
wisdom and courage,

laughter and peace,
and the love that endures all things.

God of grace,
in whose Church there is one Lord,
one Faith, one Baptism,
help us to acknowledge
that Jesus Christ is Lord,
to profess with our whole lives
the one true faith,
and to live in love and unity
with all who are baptised in his name,
through Jesus Christ our Lord,
who lives and reigns,
and is worshipped and glorified,
with you, Father, and the Holy Spirit,
one God for ever.   **Amen.**

Our Father . . .

In addition, the following may be used:

Gracious God,
touch us all again this day
with the grace of our baptism.
Give us new lives for old,
new spirits, new faith, new commitment,
in place of all that has grown tired and stale
and dead in our lives.
So may we rise and go from here,
to whatever awaits us, in joy and trust.

Eternal God,
we rejoice in the communion of all the saints,
and remember with thanksgiving
those who have already passed through
the waters of death into life eternal.

May we follow them,
faithfully and expectantly,
in the strength of our baptism
in Christ Jesus our Lord,
who lives and reigns,
and is worshipped and glorified
with you, Father, and the Holy Spirit,
one God for ever.   **Amen.**

11   *The rest of the service follows.*

C. Vows and Charge to the Congregation for Use at Confirmation

Authorised by the General Assembly of 1996

(These may replace the sections on the vows of baptismal candidates and the commitment of the congregation in the Adult Baptism and Confirmation services in *Common Order*, pp. 104 and 117.)

We ask you now to pledge yourself to a life of Christian discipleship.

Do you promise to follow Jesus Christ in your daily life?

> **With God's help**
> **I will seek to follow Christ,**
> **and in listening for God's Word,**
> **in the breaking of bread, and prayer,**
> **to grow ever closer to him as the years pass.**

Do you promise to be a faithful member of the Christian community?

> **With God's help**
> **I will share in the worship and service of the**
> **Church,**
> **and in this I will give generously**
> **of what I am and what I have.**

Do you promise to take your part in God's mission to the world?

> **With God's help**
> **I will witness to Christ**
> **wherever I find myself**

**and putting my trust and hope in him
I will seek justice and peace
and the renewing of all life
according to God's promise.**

[*or the responses may be put in the form of questions by
the minister – for example, 'Do you promise, with God's
help ...?', the candidate answering: 'With God's help I
will'.*]

*The minister then gives a charge to the congregation in
such words as:*

I charge you,
the people of this congregation,
to love, encourage and support
these our brothers and sisters in faith,
that *they* may continue to grow
in the grace of the Lord Jesus Christ
and the knowledge and love of God.

The congregation responds:

**With God's help
we will live out our baptism
as a loving community in Christ:
nurturing one another in faith,
upholding one another in prayer,
and encouraging one another in service.**

D. Hymns and Songs

Common Ground

4 'All are welcome' *the importance of all ages together and the special contribution of the young* [*CH4* 198]

18 'Come all you people' *a resounding song of thanksgiving, from Psalm 100* [*CH4* 757]

23 'Come and gather round' *the special contribution of children* [*CH4* 342]

42 'God to enfold you' *a blessing*

65 'Jesu tawa pano' *a simple affirmation of Christ's presence* [*CH4* 773]

81 'Loving Spirit' *the protection of the Holy Spirit is like a mother and father* [*CH4* 597]

83 'May the Lord' *a blessing* [*CH4* 787]

91 'Now go in peace' *a blessing* [*CH4* 789]

97 'Oh the life of the world' *all we give thanks for, including the birth of a child* [*CH4* 141]

109 'She comes' *the humility and the wonder of the child helps us understand the Spirit*

121 'The peace of the earth' *a blessing* [*CH4* 798]

122 'Take this moment' *the little child in me* [*CH4* 501]

Church Hymnary: Fourth Edition (CH4)

97 'O God, you search me' *singing version of Psalm 139 (one of the readings)*

204 'I am the Church!' *children's hymn expressing young and old in church*

632 'Our children, Lord' *reference to Mark 10 passage*

684 'The Lord created families' *families showing what welcome means*

685 'For everyone born' *a place for young and old*

686 'How happy are all' *wisdom guiding the young*
687 'Lord of our growing years' *maturing through to old age*
688 'By cool Siloam's shady rill' *reference to presentation of child Jesus in Temple*
692 'Jesus puts this song into our hearts' *and teaches us how to be a family*
696 'We come, dear Lord' *creating a welcoming home*
732 'When Jesus longed for us to know' *refers to Mark 10 passage*
786 'May the God of peace' *blessing to 'Ae Fond Kiss'*

Recorded music

Sounds of the Eternal: J. Philip Newell, soloist Suzanne Adam *meditative chants and prayers*
www.jphilipnewell.com

CDs based on CH4

Shout for Joy: 'Hymns of the Holy Spirit from *CH4*'
   'Jesus puts this song into our hearts' (see above *CH4* 692)
   'For everyone born' (see above *CH4* 685)
   'May the God of peace' (see above *CH4* 786)

Touch the earth lightly[5]
   'When Jesus longed for us to know' (see above *CH4* 732)

A taste of the Church Hymnary[5]
   'I am the Church!' (see above *CH4* 204)
   'Jesus loves me' *well-known traditional children's hymn*

5. These two CDs are out of print. Material from them will be incorporated on three forthcoming CDs based on *CH4*.

Common Ground CD

Hymns and Songs from Common Ground (out of print)
'Come all you people' (18)
'Loving Spirit' (81)
'Now go in peace' (91)
'The peace of the earth' (121)

Wild Goose CDs

Psalms of David and Songs of Mary
'The Presentation'   *Jesus as a boy taken to the Temple*
'The Rejection'   *Jesus leaves his family*

Many and Great
'Jesu, tawa pano' (see above *CG* 65)
and other tracks

There is one among us
'The peace of the earth' (see above *CG* 121)
and other tracks

Come all you people
'Pour out'   *young and old shall dream dreams*
'Come all you people' (see above *CG* 18)

E. Other Publications on Baptism

from the Office for Worship and Doctrine

wordoc@cofscotland.org.uk
0131-225 5722 ext. 359

Christian Baptism

A pamphlet in the *Common Order* series, giving a brief outline and explanation of the services. It is intended for giving to families and to those seeking baptism for themselves, and includes information about the ceremony, eligibility for baptism, useful hints on appropriate dress, what papers are required, whether videos can be made and so on.

Single copies are £1.50 from Christian bookshops, but bulk orders can be sent from the Office at a cost of 60p per copy for twenty-five or more copies.

By Water and the Spirit

This unique publication offers a composite child/adult baptism with confirmation/admission to the Lord's Supper order of service on the left-hand page and a commentary in three 'modes' on the facing pages. One strand explores the theological and liturgical significance of what is happening at each point in the service; a second offers pertinent quotations from a recent General Assembly report on Baptism; while a third makes 'suggestions for performance'. It is published by the Office for Worship and Doctrine through Saint Andrew Press.

Report of the Panel on Doctrine on Baptism

This is the text of the report to the General Assembly of 2003, when changes were made to the Act anent Baptism. It can be found in the Reports of the General Assembly 2003, page 13/1, but it is also available in desktop form from the Office for Worship and Doctrine.